Letters
from Grandpa

Tim Weaver

Production and Design: By the Book Design and Book Management and Madison Lux.

Cover art by Katharine Powell.

Cover Art: property of By The Book Design and Book Management.

Contents

Dedication

I would like to dedicate this little book, hopefully the first of various others to come, to my wonderful wife Barbara, who would always encourage me to pray and ask God to help us make a difference in the lives of the people we love, and spend time with, especially our children and our grandchildren. I thank my Lord for a second chance in life, with a helpmate of my dreams, who is known and loved by all in our great big family as Nana.

Acknowledgements

First of all, I must thank Scott and Da'Laine Hardy, for editing and advising me on biblical scripture. Scott was so very helpful in so many ways as he shared memories of his family and made suggestions pertaining to my publication. Scott also allowed me to read a couple of letters in our Sunday school class. Notable among the folks in the Sunday school class is Larry Garrett, who said, "You should put the letters in a book and publish it." Also, Willie Morse, who looked at me and nodded his head. Barbara and I are so blessed by all the friends and neighbors that the Lord has brought into our lives. I owe a special gratitude to all my church friends. I cannot leave out Kelly and Preston Condra, who inspired me after attending one of their seminars on how to witness to others, and who have published several books to assist Christians in witnessing and studying the Bible. Also, I must mention my son, Zac Weaver, who is now known as "Jude's dad" in the arena of the basketball stomping ground. Zac suggested that based on the content of my letters, the grandkids should be at least 12 years old before receiving one. Most importantly, I thank God for bringing to mind my past experiences and helping me put it down on paper.

Letter 1

Hey Jude,

Hope you are doing well, and having a happy birthday. You're twelve, right? Just messing with you. Please write back and explain what your plans are for the layoff, due to Covid 19.

You know, Jude, Barbara and I almost got stranded at the airport on our return flight when we went to visit Morgan and Nichi in Utah on Spring Break. In fact, our flight was canceled and I told Barbara, "I guess we will be spending an extended period of time with the Gomez family." Barbara turned around and said, "I hope we don't wear out our welcome." Fortunately, with the help of a stranger who was on the same flight, we were able to calm her down, and the airlines combined our flight with another due to all the cancellations.

Getting back to you. What do you plan to do with your time during days off due to no school? You know I asked Gabby the same question. She mentioned practicing basketball and soccer. Her plan was to gain ground on her teammates during the break, which at the time was only predicted to be a couple of weeks. After we got back to Norman, I called Morgan to let him know that we made it home OK. Gabby got on the phone and told me her school was closed and she was out for the rest of the year. She also said, "My dad is going to train me and three boys on Mondays, Wednesdays, and Fridays before he goes to work." This meant she would have to get up at 6:30 A.M.

Well, Mr. Jude, I hope you guys stay safe and that you take care of Eve and Flora as a big brother should. Also remember, pertaining to Jonas, my brother is thirteen years older than me. Thus, all my life I've had the same perspective as Jonas does, with you being his big brother. Today he lives in northern California and just turned 83 years old. He's about 6' 2" now, but when he was younger, he was 6' 3 ½". He played basketball and baseball, and while he was in high school, he was MVP in both sports his senior year. He didn't play in college due to the fact his girlfriend was going to have a baby. As it turned out, he dropped out of college (University of Tulsa), became a dad, married his girlfriend, and got a job (not necessarily in that order). When I was in junior high and discovered girls, he told me that I should take my time and stay off the phone with girls. He kept saying, "There's plenty of time in your life for girls. You should concentrate on your school work and sports." He also told me that Mom taught him how to handle the bad times he faced with prayer: asking God to help him with things he would go through in his young life, like when our grandpa died, problems at school, getting along with coaches, teammates, playing time when he was a freshman, etc. *He went on to say that it was when things were going great that he messed up the most.*

Anyway Jude, with all the free time I hope you are able to write me a short letter.

Love U,

Grandpa

Letter 2

Dear Jude,

Here goes my second letter to my oldest grandson. Last time I shared a story about my older brother, who played baseball in the summer and basketball in the winter.

This time I'm thinking it would be good to share about your Aunt Morgan and her time of playing basketball in junior high and high school. As you know she played for Norman High. At the time she played, the city of Norman only had one high school (six A). They won the state championship her junior and senior years. All of the starters on the team went D 1. We're talking Stanford University, Connecticut, OU, TU, etc. In high school, Morgan was a starter about 25% of the time. She was considered the sixth player. She was always one of the first players to come off the bench. As I look back, I can remember a time when she was great in practice and home games, but would be nervous pertaining to end of the season tournaments. She would play stiff, not relaxed, you know, trying not to make a mistake and the more I said the worse it got. I couldn't keep quiet, just trying to help my little girl, because I knew and had witnessed how good she could be. On the way home I would say you feel OK and she would look at me and say, "Dad, if I make a mistake, then I'm on the bench."

Jude, you are not going to believe this: Morgan just called to wish me a happy Father's

Day, and I explained to her that I was in the process of writing you a letter. In the letter I was referring to her basketball playing days in high school. Also, being specific about what I was writing about, like being nervous in the state tournament. She said, "Oh yeah, I remember those days." She then went on to say that Nichie was coaching a 9th grade boy with the same problem. Practice, Super Star, hitting every shot. Recreational league, Super Star, hitting shots, great passes, etc. School team great player, but when he gets picked for an all select tournament team with players that he's never played with, he's off his game. Nichie would say to him, "What's up with you? You've got the best release shot on the team. Shoot The Ball." After the game he said, "Coach, I was afraid if I missed, then you would set me down...right in front of my parents and their friends who came to watch me play."

So, Niche says to him, "Well if you are worried about going down, let me tell you this: If you go down, don't go down for a bad pass. Don't go down for a turnover or being out of position. Go down because you missed three or four shots in a roll. As a coach, most likely I will not take you out if you are taking good shots at the basket…SO, SHOOT THE BALL WHEN YOU'RE NERVOUS."

Sincerely yours,

Grandpa

Letter 3

Dear Jude, Gabby, Fuller, Spencer, & Eve,

I'm sure that by now everyone has heard that Jude got a car. That's right; at 16 years old Jude has become mobile, and if you do not like the way he drives then maybe you should stay off the sidewalks. Seriously, my prayer is that Jude will be very cautious while driving in Houston.

As your grandpa, I thought that I would share with you when I acquired my first car at 16 years old. Actually, my dad and mom purchased my first car. It was a 1956 two-door

Chevrolet with a six-cylinder engine and a three-speed standard shift transmission. It had about a 120 horsepower. The color of my car was baby blue with white stripes.

Well, I was very excited about my car. The only thing was that some of my friends were getting their first car too. Many of them were being presented with or surprised by their parents with sporty, cool, fast automobiles, and almost all were later models than my car. Nevertheless, I turned sixteen on March the 22nd and was ready to drive!

Summer break was only like 5 or 6 weeks away, so I began to think, "What can I do to make my car look better?" There was this older kid who had some mag wheels for sale that would fit my car. Mag wheels are manufactured from alloys containing mainly magnesium. The only thing was he wanted $300 for his wheels. Prior to this, I thought that I would never have a car at 16 years old, so I had dropped out of sports and taken a part time job after school to save money. It turned out to be a bad move for me, because after weeks of working after school I didn't have enough money to buy the wheels for a car which I already had, thanks to my parents. I became obsessed with how I could acquire those wheels—which would solve my problem and move my car to the next level of cool, and being admired by my friends.

How do I get those wheels? That was the three hundred dollar question. As mentioned, I had a part time job, but I didn't make enough money to buy the wheels anytime soon. The truth was the summer would probably be almost over before I could save enough money to purchase the wheels. I didn't even have a savings account like some of my friends. Then it came to me, "I'll go to the bank and borrow the money and pay it back with the money I make each week from my job." Great idea, I thought. At least it was worth a try rather than doing nothing. The next day I left school early in order to go to the bank before work. I had rehearsed what I would say to the bank person, loan officer, or whomever. I would explain that I have a job and will pay the money back at $50 a month until all is paid back to the bank. The bank I went to is where my parents banked and when I told the man my name, he confirmed that he knew my parents. After explaining my plan for borrowing the money, to my surprise he said, "Sure, we can loan you the money." After filing out a paper with the amount, he presented it to me for my signature and I signed it. He then said, "You will need your dad to sign also," and showed me where he should sign. I'm not sure if he could tell by the look on my face that my brain just went into neutral. This was indeed a major roadblock for my plans. Later, I understood that this was called co-signing or surety. My dad co-signing the note for my loan made him the surety for the loan. In other words, If I was unable to pay the loan back to the bank, they would come after my dad. Great, that's just great. What now? My reasoning and past experience in trying to persuade my dad to do something of this nature was: "HE WILL NEVER SIGN THIS GUARANTEE FOR MY LOAN!!" And if I ask him, he will just say "NO!", and that will be the end of it. The money was practically in my hand; I could picture the wheels on my car. Now the question was, "How do I get him to sign?" I want you guys to know that this is a true story and this is where it gets a little embarrassing for me to continue, but here it goes. Have you ever had a parent say to you, "Young man or young lady you need to clean your room?" Well, as a young man, I began to ponder and scheme on how I could be successful in bringing this about—my dad co-signing.

I was thinking on how I was always bringing home papers from school for my parents to sign pertaining to field trips, sports participation, etc. It just so happened that I had something from school which I needed one of them to sign. Again, this is hard for me as a grandpa to confess…I began to scheme and calculate my next move. I know! I will include the note for the loan in with the school stuff to be signed. Once more, every time I tell this story I feel so remorseful and want to tell you guys what a mischievous brat that I was. You may ask yourselves, "Was this the right thing to do? That would be a resounding NO! But the confession continues; As I waited for my dad to come out of the shower in his underwear without his glasses, holding paper and pen in hand I said, "Dad, you need to sign these papers for school." I think he said, "Let me get my glasses." I told another lie: "Dad, I'm in a hurry," as I put my finger on the line and held the paper to the bathroom door. My trusting dad signed the papers, including the bank note for the $300 loan.

The next day I took the paper to the bank, and the loan officer said, "I was hoping to see you and your dad." Thus, I told another lie: he couldn't make it, had to work late or something. He said, "That's OK, I'll be right back after I verify your dad's signature." He soon returned with $300 cash and had me sign a couple of papers on receiving the money. After a little talk about me starting a savings account with the bank, out the door with the money I went, headed to purchase the wheels for my car.

About three or four years later, when I was a freshman at Oklahoma State University, I was at home for Christmas break and having a leisurely conversation with my mom. I began to tell the story about how I truly got the wheels for my first car. You see, I did purchase the wheels. I installed them on my car and was able to make payments and pay off the loan to the bank. When I explained to my mom that dad unknowingly co-signed for my loan, I noticed fear came over her face. She listened and stared intently at me. She said, "Oh heavens, if your dad had found out, he would have killed you!" She went on to say, "Do not ever share this story with anyone else." The year was December 1970. My dad died almost 20 years later at 89, and my mom insisted that it would not be wise to ever tell him. "It would only hurt him," she said. So, my dad never knew how I deceived him on that day.

What I didn't realize is that I had created debts that I couldn't pay. My wages were about $1.60 per hour at my part time job. I had broken the 5th commandment in the Bible, God's Holy Word, which says, "Honor your father and your mother." Honor means to love and respect them, not deceive and disrespect them. Also, by lying to my parents and the banker, I had broken the 9th commandment in the Bible, God's Holy Word, which is "Thou Shalt Not Lie." Because of my actions and other choices I made as a young man, my sin debt was devastating! The Bible says, "For the wages of sin is death." (Romans 6:23) The problem was, this time I couldn't pay it back, no matter how good I would be the for rest of my life or how hard I would work in helping others. It did not matter how much money I would give to the poor or to the church. My parents had taken me to church as a youngster and I had a little knowledge of the Bible. I had attended Bible School in the summers. I was a member of the church and had attended Sunday School with my friends almost every Sunday. I remembered that the Bible teaches that God is just, and history reveals that God always punishes those who sin. In addition, I was completely mentally aware that I was of that sort. A Sinner…! The question was, "What do I do now?" Who is Jesus really, and what does it mean to be saved? What has Jesus done for me? Everyone says that the Bible is all about Jesus. Keep your eyes on Jesus. What would Jesus do? Jesus sets the example. Jesus loves you. How can I have a personal relationship with the King of Kings, Savior of the world?

If you have broken God's law, you need Jesus…. There is no other way. See John 14:6. Jesus is the only way to be made righteous before God. Righteous means to be made right with God Almighty—to be able to stand in the righteousness of Jesus Christ on judgment day. See Hebrews 9:27. Where will you spend Eternity? Jesus will become the Surety for your Sin Debt. Believe in Him, and Jesus Will Save You. If you have broken God's Law as I did, you need Jesus. Jesus took our punishment for sinning and paid for it by dying on the cross and rising from the dead 2000 years ago. We must believe that the Bible is True and place our Faith in Him Alone for Salvation (1 Corinthians 15:1-4). When Jesus had by himself purged our sins, he sat down on the right hand of The Majesty on High (Hebrews 1:3, Mark 12:36).

Love,

Grandpa

Letter 4

Jude, Gabby, Fuller, Spencer, & Eve,

Buenos Noches,

Here's a question for you. Have you ever helped someone? As in the past, I ask the same question to myself. Have I ever helped someone by giving my time or something without expecting anything in return? I am going back to when I was a teen or preteen. There was that time when my cousins and I would help our grandpa, which included digging with a shovel and moving rocks. I remember our parents asking, "Were the boys any help?" My grandpa replied, "When you have one boy helping, normally you have a whole boy. When you have two boys helping you end up with half a boy." He was referring to our goofing off and horseplay. I have heard older people add, "When you have three boys, you don't have any boy at all."

Personally, I feel that the previous paragraph holds a lot of truth. An example would be when Gibson comes over to practice his hitting, it normally goes pretty smooth and he gets in a lot of swings. On the other hand, when his friend Henry comes with him, it's totally different with a ton of distractions and horseplay, etc. As for me, I like it either way, just wanting them to have fun and enjoy each other's company. After all they are just little boys…

Sorry, kind of got off track. So, let's get back

to the question: Have I ever helped someone? There was a time when I was in the 9th grade, I started the year at a new school. It was kinda tough for me because I didn't know anyone at this school. After one year I was able to transfer back to my old school where I knew almost everyone, with friends, etc. Like I said, I really didn't look forward to going to this new school. In fact, no one hardly even spoke to me.

After about two or three weeks at this new school, there was this one kid who would talk to me in class. I considered him to be my friend, in fact, my only friend. He was Latino, and I got the feeling that his parents didn't have a lot of money based on the clothes he wore. I noticed that he wore the same clothes several days in a row. One day I told him that I had some clothes at home that were too big for me, and maybe they would fit his older brothers. Actually, I didn't even know if he had an older brother and he was about my size. Anyway, he said, "That would be good; thank you." After he took the clothes a couple of days later, I noticed he was wearing them, and to my surprise, they fit perfectly. When we talked about it, he said his mother altered them for him. In summary, when I think about when I was young and all the stupid stuff I did and said, remembering things like this makes me feel good.

In the Bible, Jesus speaks on helping others in Matthew 25:34-40. It's just seven verses, and I implore you to read them…Know that I love you and pray for you every day.

Yours truly,

Grandpa

Letter 5

Dear Jude, Gabby, Fuller, Spencer, & Eve,

This letter is about prayer. Prayer is the simplest act of soliciting God, to ask or request something. You do not need learning, wisdom, or book knowledge. Prayer is simply speaking to God in your own words and in your own way, and all you need is heart and will. Think of a child when they take their first step and how excited the parents are, as they share this special event with friends and family. I wonder if God and the angels celebrate this moment in heaven when a person prays for the first time?

When my dad died, my uncle told me that he was saved and we will see him again in Heaven. My uncle Milton was a song leader in a small country church where we sometimes attended. Dad would go on occasion if my mom pressured him. As mentioned before, we lived on a dairy farm which required a lot of work. In addition to the responsibility of the farm, my dad also worked 40 hours a week at a steel foundry in Tulsa. OK, getting back to when my uncle told me that my dad was saved…He went on to say that one time after church, he confronted my dad about accepting Jesus as his savior. He said, "Your dad explained, 'I'm already saved.'" My uncle Milton said to my dad, "I do not remember you coming forward in church and praying with the preacher." My dad told him it didn't happen in church. That's when my uncle Milton said, "OK, tell me when and where it happened." My dad told him, some time back, there was a week in his life where nothing went right, with one problem after the other. Tractors would not start, the car had a flat tire, plumbing problems at the house, and the animals were unwilling to do what they had done every day for years pertaining to going into their stalls to be fed and hooked up to the milkers, etc. He went on to say that one day he was chasing a young heifer when he fell down in the mud and the cow manure, where he said, "Please Lord, forgive me and save me from a devil's hell." You must understand my dad, (your great grandpa) was born in 1912, and it was definitely a different era in history... In summary, that little prayer changed his life.

Another example of a short prayer and a person's life being changed happened to a young man not too long ago. He explained that he was having issues with his friends, his parents, his teachers, and his coaches...

When one thing would be resolved something else would pop up…He went to a youth rally with a friend. The speaker said, "if you have a personal relationship with Jesus, He will share your burdens." That night while lying in bed looking up at the ceiling, he turned over, and in all sincerity, he prayed, "Jesus, if you are real then please be real to me."

In summary, it all starts with prayer, and you must do it for yourself. No one can do it for you…see James 4:2&3. The preeminent fact about both of the true stories pertaining to my dad and the young man is something I found out later. The one common denominator is that people were praying for them…

Please know, that Nanna and I love you and pray for you every day.

Love,

Grandpa

Letter 6

Dear Jude, Gabby, Fuller,

This will be the first letter for the year of 2023. You guys are always on my mind, and I was thinking the other day about how many things you all have in common with each other. For example, all of you are the oldest sibling in your family. Also, it's pretty neat that you all play basketball on a high level. You are all teenagers, and you are all slower than me. ☺ It's amazing how many things that you have in common with each other, and I've just mentioned a few of them. It is easy to see that all of you have improved your game over the years that I have been watching you play. I must confess that basketball has always been one of my favorite sports to watch and play, except for baseball. I can remember when my parents would take me to my older brother's basketball games. If you would like a perception of what that would look like, think about Jonas watching Jude play, for the age difference is exactly the same.

A long time ago, there was this kid in my Sunday School class that I taught; I'm thinking he was about in the eighth grade. He had a favorite basketball player that he knew everything about. I mean everything. He knew his parents' names. He knew the high school he went to, that he played basketball for North Caralina, and that he was drafted by the Chicago Bulls. He knew all of his statistics and much more. The player's name is Michael

Jordan. We confronted him and asked, "Does Michael Jordan know you?" The kid just looked at us with kind of a funny look on his face. Another kid said, "If Michael Jordan walked in the door would he know you?" The young man reluctantly said, "No, he would not know me."

Something came to mind, and I explained that we have been studying the Bible and we know everything, well maybe not everything, but a lot about Jesus. The question is, if He walked in the door, would He know any of us? The Bible mentions a book called, "The Book of Life." Someone asked, "Is your name written in the Lamb's Book of Life?" A man by the name of John saw Jesus walking one day and said, "Behold the Lamb of God." (John 1:29)

In conclusion, this means that Jesus has a book called the Book of Life, which will have all the names of the believers written in it. Always remember, Christianity is a relationship, not a religion.

Yours truly,

Grandpa

Letter 7

To: Jude, Gabby, Fuller,

This letter, is a continuation of the previous letter in which it was discussed all the things you 3 have in common. One example being that the sport of basketball is played at a high level by all of you in relation to your age group. As mentioned, improvement in your game and your basketball IQ is very noticeable. Better performance is sure to come when you play and practice a lot.

Now, let me ask you a question. Do you know the rules when it comes to the game of basketball? Let me answer that for you. Pretty much, of course you do. Have you ever been called for walking, stepping out of bounds, crossing the free throw line too early, backcourt violation, etc.? I am sure that you have been called for a contact foul. By the way, most players do not like a quick whistle by the referees. One often hears from the spectators in the stands, "That's Not a Foul!" "Let Them Play!" "Enough of The Touch Fouls!" OK, here's another question for you: If someone tells you that it's OK for a player on offense to stay in the lane for three minutes you would say, "That's False! A player on offense can only stay in the lane 3 seconds."

There was a very successful basketball coach. You might say, "He was the General of the team," which included assistant coaches, support staff, player development, video coordinator, recruiting coordinator, graduated assistants, student managers, ball boys, etc. The General had started out as a private, a player in training, who came up through the ranks, all the way, and is now a General, in charge of the team. At the first of the season the coach had a list of 28 players. The list included walk-ons as well partial scholarship and full scholarship players. Due to the coach's background and history, he could relate to what his subordinates were striving to achieve. As mentioned, there were 28 players on the list, but only 15 dressed out for a game. All of the players had exceptional talent or they would not have been on a D1 team. Each player had a certain gift or ability that they exceled in; examples were rebounding, blocking out, assists, excellent passer, ball handler, few turnovers, stealing the ball, anticipating and intercepting a pass, scoring, taking the ball to the basket, shooting the ball, etc.

This particular year the team had been very successful. The coach felt that this team was one with better than average talent. In fact, he had 8 or 9 players that he could sub in and out of a game with no drop-off pertaining to defense or offense. He decided to go off the grid a bit, or in other words, deviate a little in following the tried-and-true coaching techniques of the game. The season was almost over with two games left on their schedule before their conference tournament and then "The Big Dance." His plan, was to call each player into his office and place the team roster before them, asking the player to circle four players on the roster they would want to go into battle with in order to win the championship. The coach felt it would help him tweak the team pertaining to optimal chemistry of the players who would be on the floor at any given time. Players that place their teammates as a valued significance to the overall success of the team.

In summary, they did go all the way and successfully completed an undefeated season winning the championship. When the General was interviewed during the postgame and was asked about his assistant coaches and the success of his players, he replied, "They were swift and sure in a pressure type of defense and very determined on offense." He went on to say, "They were modest and restrained in victory." He said, "I don't know what they would have been in defeat, Because They Never Lost A GAME!" After his statement, the fans Exploded in such Jubilation and Celebration…

OK, now we are really going to change gears here…Let me ask you this question, "Do you know what to do, and how to live your life, in order to spend forever in Heaven in the next life?" For millions of people believe that there is indeed life after death. The unexpected concept for me, when I was your age, was the fact that in this nation we have freedom of religion. It gives us, as citizens of the United States of America, the right to practice whatever religion we choose. We also have freedom of speech which allows individuals to express themselves without government interference or regulation. As mentioned, millions of people believe in life after death but they differ on how one is to get to Heaven. The Teachers, Preachers, Pastors, Priests, Rabbis, Ministers, Imams, Parsons, Clergymen, Clergywomen, Televangelist etc., may insist that they have the truth on how to spend eternity with God in Heaven…If you do not read your Bible, then it will be hard to know what's true or false. *Someone may say,"* *It's OK to spend 3 minutes in the lane."* **That's False!!!** *Who says?* **It is written in the rule** *book an offensive player cannot be in the lane for more than 3 seconds while his team has control of the ball. Remember, The Truth Is Still The Truth, Even If No One Believes It. A Lie Is Still A Lie, Even If Everyone Believes It.*

If you want to know how to get a grip on life and Stuff! your adversary when he tries to slam dunk you, remember what Jesus said… It Is Written. **READ** Luke 4:3-12. Also, do not be swayed from the Truth…**READ** 2nd Peter 3:16-17.

Yours truly,

Grandpa

Letter 8

Hola! Jude, Gabby, Fuller, Spencer, & Eve,

I know it seems like the summer is just flying by. Did you know that the days start getting shorter on June the 21st? Also, July the 4th is just around the corner. Are you guys looking forward to fun at The Four Seasons in Dallas or maybe Camp Kanakuk?

Well, the question for this time is what do you fear? As always, let me ask myself this question, "What do I fear or what did I fear as a teenager?" As mentioned before, there was the time when we moved from a rural farm to the city. My class went from 14 to over 500 students, which meant leaving friends behind and hoping to make new ones. For some this comes easy, making friends that is. For me, it was like one friend would lead to two friends and two friends would lead to three friends, etc. I said all this to try and explain that one of my fears as a teenager was being rejected or not being included in the so-called friend circle. I remember that I had church friends, because we always went to church with our parents. I had school friends, baseball team friends, basketball team friends, Boy Scout friends, and there were always neighborhood friends. In conclusion, the more exposure, the more friends. You know, I still have friends from elementary school, high school, and college that I so appreciate. When we get together, it's so good to reminisce about the past. Even when we have not seen each other for years, the childhood friendship comes to the surface immediately. It's grounding, and for me, I consider it to be the best therapy a person can receive, like a phenomenon or reality to experience over and over in your life. Like people say, "You can make friends, but you can't make old friends". Although, there is one exception, and His name is Jesus, who has always been there for you, even when you were formed in the womb. (Psalm 139:13-14)

I went on Google and asked the question, "What's the number one fear of teenagers today, in the whole world?" Number one is losing a friend due to some type of tragedy. We also have less serious fears. For me, when I was a teenager, I had a nervous fear of speaking to a large audience. My fear was enhanced when at the end of my speech or presentation the audience was allowed to ask questions. I found that the more I did something, the less fear I had. It was like making a free throw when the game was on the line or coming to bat with two outs in the bottom of the ninth inning. In my experience, when you do something over and over, the fear goes away and you actually look forward to it.

In summary, how can I offer you advice that may help you to be successful in life? Know that this advice comes from someone who loves you without limit. My first advice would be that you be careful who you allow to influence your life. Today's world is different in some ways compared to the world I grew up in. You guys have constant and instant communication. Fads pop up almost every week and it's easy to become enamored with a trending fad or something that's going on, but when I do that, I'm allowing somebody that I don't know and who probably does not have my best interest at heart to influence my thoughts, my behavior, and my beliefs. When this happens, it has a significant impact on your character and your personal culture.

In closing, in the Bible there's a story of a young man who became very apprehensive about his future, when he became king of a nation at only 19 or 20 years old. I encourage you to read King Solomon's prayer, 1 Kings 3:4-9. In my opinion you should not put a whole lot of faith in man's prediction of the future. For it is true wisdom to recognize that God controls the future, be it an individual or a nation. Your past may have consequences, but it does not control your future.

Sincerely,

Grandpa

Letter 9

To: Jude, Gabriella, Fuller, Spencer, & Eve,

The subject of this letter is maturity.

When I taught Sunday school for the 7th and 8th grade, our classroom was next to the 5th grade classroom. At times, the 5th grade boys would run by our room, being loud and disruptive. It really didn't bother me like it did some of the other teachers. In fact, at this church most of our Sunday school teachers were also teachers in our public schools. They expected respect and order. My take on the situation was understanding that kids will be kids, and I actually wanted them to have fun in church but most importantly learn about Jesus. One time, when these fifth-grade boys were running in the hallway, I stopped them and asked, "Do you boys know the difference between 5th graders and 7th graders?" They kinda wobbled their heads, meaning no. I told them, "5th graders run in the hallway and 7th graders do not, so try to be more mature, like 7th graders." They smiled at me and went on their way.

What about becoming a mature Christian? Some of you just got back from Camp Kanakuk and POW!!—it's time to start a new school year, with a completely different atmosphere. What I remember most about my school days was going from junior high to high school, which was in a completely different part of town. The summer had ended and it was time to be reunited with your friends, but now we are all in high school, feeling some of them had changed, being more mature you might say. While others were still the same, cracking jokes, making fun of each other with put downs, just like our junior high years. In the Bible, it talks about being a mature believer. (1 Corinthians 3:1-3) It starts out with the preacher saying, "I could not address you as mature Christians but as baby Christians." I encourage you to read the three verses.

Mature Christians say if you read your Bible and Pray for Wisdom, Knowledge, and Understanding, you will have discernment when it comes to making decisions and choices pertaining to your future success in life. In this world, you will find that it's a battle for your mind, and it's becoming harder to find the Truth when making a decision or a choice. I find that there's two sides that seem to always have different consequences. The deceiver only portrays the good side, thus hiding the bad side. Also, it can be very painful and expensive to learn the hard way, and believe me, I can attest to that.

I hope you will read your Bible, Pray, and hold on to the feeling you had at camp Kanakuk. Do not worry. Do not judge. Do not be all about yourself.

Yours Truly,

Grandpa

Letter 10

Dear Jude, Gabby, Fuller, Spencer, & Eve,

Hello again! I thought I would share another story of when I was young. When I was born, my parents lived on a dairy farm. My brother and I went to a small country school. Gene, my older brother, was a freshman at the University of Tulsa when I started the first grade, and Ted was in kindergarten. My younger brother and I always did stuff together on the farm due to the fact that our closest neighbor was 3 miles away. We were very close in age, only 14 months apart. Also, Ted was bigger than me. In fact, some of the kids would ask who is the older. Later in life, I asked my mom why I was the smallest compared to my brothers. She said that when she was pregnant with me, she smoked cigarettes, but with Gene and Ted she did not. Our farm was located along the Arkansas River near Sand Springs, Oklahoma. When the Keystone Lake was built, it took our farm, and we moved to Sand Springs. It was at this time that things became very different between my brother and I. Our neighborhood was full of kids, so we still did stuff together but less due to the fact that he had his friends, and I had mine.

We seemed to fight a lot, because he would get into my stuff. I'm sure I would ignore him when he would warn me to leave his stuff alone. There were times when we would actually have hitting fights. Harsh words were exchanged and our relationship began to break down and deteriorate. One time when he was 13 and I was 14, we had a fight because Ted had taken off on my scooter without asking me. Our mom came out and made us stop fighting. She turned to me and said, "I want to talk to you now, in the house." She was always talking to me after Ted and I would have a confrontation due to the fact that I was the oldest. She would always rebuke me, like I should know proper conduct, being older. Of course, I would interrupt her and plead my case, i.e., he broke it or he messed it up some way. She would explain how silly and inappropriate it was to fight over stuff. She would remind me that he would always be my brother, but the scooter will be history in a couple of years. You know, she was right! In less than two years I turned 16 and gotten my first car.

As I got older, my mom became wiser in my eyes. In fact, I have experienced the feeling of remorse because I did not pay more attention to her advice when I was a teenager. As a young man, I realized that some of her wisdom had rubbed off on me. I am thankful to be able to remember some of the times she tried to correct my thinking, my attitude, and my actions.

The Bible says in Proverbs 9:7-8, "Anyone who rebukes a mocker will get an insult in return and anyone who corrects the wicked will get hurt." So, don't bother correcting mockers; they will only hate you.

The dictionary defines a mocker or scoffer as people who defy and renounce truth and good advice, not only to their own detriment and destruction but also that of others.

Yours Truly, with all my love,

Grandpa

P.S. The story that you just read is true, to the best of my recollection. Also, I believe, as do millions, that the Bible is The Truth.

Letter 11

Dear Spencer,

I was trying to decide what should I write in a letter to you. Well, let's see, you are twelve years old. I will try to go back in time to when I was twelve years old and try to recall what my interest and activities were.

Ok, we are talking 60 years ago when I was twelve. My family had just moved from a dairy farm in the country, where our closest neighbor was about three miles away, to Sand Springs, Oklahoma. My younger brother was in the 4th grade and I was in the 5th. Now let me think what were my interest and what occupied my time…Let's see, there was school, and spending time with my friends, which took up about 50%. Also, there was basketball and fall league baseball. I definitely always looked forward to summer, because it was fun, fun, fun! I remember having so much fun in the summer, except when I had to get up early to throw my paper route. That's right, I had to get up at 5 A.M. to deliver the morning papers and got paid about $35.00 a month. There was a saying back in those days by the kids: "Paper boys always have spending money." Also, in the summer we had to mow our own lawn for free, but my brother and I got $5.00 for mowing the neighbor's lawn. We had to help our dad with whatever project he had going on for the weekend.

Now the really fun stuff to me was on week nights in the summer when we had little league baseball games. We practiced a couple of times a week, and we played our games under the lights at Pee Wee Park. It seemed like the whole town would turn out to watch us play. My brother and I played on the 14-year-old team even though he was 11 and I was 12. We always played in the outfield when we got to play. There were tons of girls that always hung around our dugout asking questions about the older boys on the team. I remember that they would call me over to the fence and give me a note to give to our pitcher or shortstop on the team. They were actually kind of a pain at times, I mostly didn't mind because before this I didn't have much to do with girls, and they were older and all fixed up…you know make up and stuff…

Oh Spencer, you will like this story, which happened later that summer. In our neighborhood, there was a family next door that had five kids. Well, there were two boys which were older, like high school, and three girls. The oldest girl was in the eighth grade and she was beautiful, especially to a twelve-year-old. Let's just say her name was Miss Pretty...the older woman. Pertaining to the other two girls, one was in the six grade and the other was in the fourth. There were always a lot of kids at their house, and we played basketball in the driveway and volleyball in their backyard. In the summer time, we got to stay out late, because it didn't get dark until like 8:30 or 9pm. Well, one evening after playing volleyball in their backyard one of the older boys said, "Let's play spin the bottle." There were a bunch of kids, both girls and boys, with me being the youngest. I had no idea how to play spin the bottle. Anyway, the rules of the game were, with everyone in a circle, a girl would spin a glass Coke bottle, and no matter which boy it pointed to or landed on she had to kiss him. Same for boys when they would spin the bottle and it landed on a girl. Thus, as the youngest, I kinda snuck in the circle to be in the game, you know, unnoticed. Lo and behold, the bottle landed on me on the first spin by Miss Pretty!!! Well, she came over to me—the kid who wasn't even a teenager—took hold of my face, turned my head and gave me a kiss on the cheek. THEN! All of a sudden, this older boy, about 14 or 15, yelled, "You can't do that! You gotta kiss him on the mouth!" (Man, was I thankful he was there!) So, she turned and kissed me right on the mouth. THIS was the first time ever in my life! WOW. Actually, as I think back, it was only a quick little peck on the lips, but being a fifth grader kissed by Miss Pretty, the eighth grader, it definitely had a major impact on me…and that was the only time that the bottle landed on me that evening. There was another time after playing volleyball. It was getting dark, and the older kids decided to play spin the bottle; but when I tried to sneak into the game, an older boy looked intently at me and said, "BEAT IT kid!" So, I didn't get to play.

Love,

Grandpa

Letter 12

Jude, Gabby, Fuller, Spencer, & Eve,

The story you are about read is true and was heard by me and others. As your grandpa, I'm putting it in a letter to you, to the best of my recollection.

There was a young married couple, and they had three children. Their first child was a boy who was eight years old and his name is Aziel, which means "God is my Helper." He had two sisters; they were five and almost two years old.

Aziel's mother began teaching her children

to pray when they were very young. Aziel had been praying with his mother every night before he would go to bed. At 8½ years old, Aziel was one of the most popular kids in his school. He was a good student and all of the teachers favored him. Math was his favorite subject, and he excelled in sports. In fact, he was one of the fasted boys in his school. His favorite sport was basketball, but he played whatever was in season. In the spring, he would play soccer and start practicing baseball. He was always one of the first players chosen and it didn't matter which sport. Aziel was so successful that all the boys wanted him as a friend and a teammate. His dad worked long hours and didn't get to attend all of his games, but his mother was always there.

Every night, Aziel would kneel with his mom to pray when she would come into his bedroom. One night his mom came into his bedroom to pray with him, and he said, "Mom I do not want to pray tonight." His mom asked, "Why do you not want to pray tonight?" Aziel told his mom, "I really don't need anything and I can't think of anything to pray for." His mom said, "OK then, let's thank God for what He has provided for you." Aziel looked at his mom and asked, "What has He provided for me?" She said, "Aziel, I'm going to check on the girls and I'll be right back, but why don't you think about what you can thank God for while I'm checking on your sisters. He said, "OK mom I'll try." His mother whispered a prayer as she was walking out of his room. (O Lord, please help us.)

When his mother returned, they began to pray and Aziel started his prayer by asking God to forgive him for not always saying or doing the right thing. Aziel began by thanking God for his mom, dad, and sisters. He then thanked God for his legs that helped him run fast. (He knew a little boy that went to his school that was in a wheelchair due to an automobile accident when he was only three years old.) He thanked the Lord for his hands that helped him catch footballs, baseballs, and basketballs. Aziel continued his prayer by thanking the Lord in an escalated voice, and "O God, thank you for my eyes that I can see." He told his mom later that he saw a blind person at the church that they attended. After Aziel had concluded his prayer, "In Jesus name, Amen." His mother said that he looked up into her eyes and his face was radiant, and he declared, "Mom, the Lord has been so good to me!"

In summary, in the Bible there are many recordings throughout history of kings, rulers, and people in high places of authority that failed to thank the God of Heaven for their success. If you would like to see their foreboding, please take time to read. I've listed one from the Old Testament and one from the New Testament. After reading, I'm sure that you will agree with me that it is of the most importance that those who are truly children of the Most High, meaning believers in His Son Jesus, should always give thanks and Glory to God for all of our blessings and success that we may have in this life. Read Daniel 4:1-37, pertaining to King Nebuchadnezzar. Also, Acts 12:20-24, about King Herod. The Bible alludes to radiant, or beaming, see Ps. 34:5 and Stephen in Acts chapter 5.

Yours Truly,

Grandpa

Letter 13

Aloha again: Jude, Gabriela, and Fuller.

Hope everything is going well for you, pertaining to school, sports, family, friends, etc. When I was your age, the anticipation of summer break was on my mind. Baseball teams had begun practicing, and I was ready for warmer weather, with no more studying for tests, and no more homework.

My question for you today is, "Who do you trust?" Maybe I should say, who do you really, really, trust? Do you trust your dad, your mom, your sister, your brother, or maybe your close friend? I asked Nana this question and her response was God. An old preacher said, "When I was a young man and had read the Bible through several times, I felt that I knew God and what he wanted for my life, but I didn't Trust him. Now that I'm an old man, I confess that I have no idea what God will do in my life, but I Trust Him."

When I was your age, I had several friends and many acquaintances, but I must divulge to you that I only truly trusted a few of my closest friends. In high school I had girlfriends that I would take to movies, out to lunch, or even dinner. When I would drive them home after the movie or whatever we would sometimes kiss goodnight. So, I guess you could say that we were close friends. Then again, I would catch some of them in lies, and would no longer trust them. This one guy who I considered a friend would ride with me to lunch in my car and sometimes we would take his car. Well, this same guy not only lied to me but stole some of my stuff. One thing that hurt me the most and angered me for sure, was when a teammate betrayed me. Some dudes became hostile toward me, and it was like he was on their side and thought it was funny that they wanted to beat me up.

There was a young man who was arrested for stealing copper wire along the railroad track in the town where he lived. He would walk along the railroad track and climb the telephone or utility poles and cut the copper ground wire. His picture showed up in the local newspaper explaining the crime he had committed and his court date.

When a wealthy real estate broker read the story about the young man, he turned to his business partner and exclaimed this is the perfect epitome of an uneducated airhead, knucklehead, or whatever you want to call him. His partner said, "Just plain stupid of him to steal copper wire from the telephone poles on the railroad track."

Together, they decided to help the young man. They managed to get him out of jail and get him cleaned up. The next day, the real estate broker took him into town and bought him new shoes and clothes. They even paid for his college education. Several years later the man who had stolen the copper wire along the railroad track became very successful as an adult. Many people referred to him as a shrewd businessman. The truth is, he was malicious, cruel, and deceptive in his dealings. It was said that he went back to his hometown where he grew up and stole the whole railroad company.

In summary, if you are indeed a child of the Most High, I encourage you to ask Him for wisdom in choosing your friends. When I was in college, I met a young man at the Baptist Student Union who told me that he would always pray, "Lord please show me this person's heart." Only God can change a person's heart. Education is good but it does not make you kind, honest, ethical, moral, or righteous…

If you want to know what to do, if in your opinion, someone does you wrong, read Luke 17:3-4.

With all my Love,

Grandpa

Letter 14

To: Jude, Gabriella, Fuller, Spencer, & Eve,

This letter Is about people that crossed my path, who I considered smarter than the average person.

Let's start off with when I graduated from Oklahoma State University. I was hired by Mobil Oil Company, which is now Exxon/Mobil. All of the new hires from the central region of the United States were sent to training school in Chicago, IL. That is where I met # 1; that is what all of us new hires called him. When the supervisor passed out our test papers from the highest score to the lowest, you guessed it, # 1 always got his first. Personally, I never received the highest or the lowest test score, always somewhere around the middle except for one #3. There were about 14 guys in the class that started in January and ran through May. I found the class much harder than courses I had taken in college—more pressure, etc. This guy from the University of Nebraska, (#1) always received his graded test paper back first with the highest test score. Not sure what happened to #1, maybe he went on to be the president of the company or something.

The following person, who I considered smart at the time, was in my freshman class at Oklahoma State, and we lived in the same dormitory. We both enrolled in R.O.T.C. (Reserved Officers Training Corps). Most all branches of the Armed Services offer this to college students, and we decided on the Army. He seemed like a nice guy from Kansas. We would walk to class together, and sit next to each other. We didn't even buy a book for the class. He said, "We should do fine by attending class and listening to the lectures." Just to let you know, after the first test I bought a book, and you will see why. Let me be clear: my friend did not have a book and did not take notes on the teacher's lectures. He just sat at his chair and seemed to be listening intently. When we took our first test, the graduate assistants passed out 4 different tests with the same questions, but in different order. This would keep you from cheating off your neighbor. Well, when we received our graded test papers back, yours truly made a C on the first test. As for my buddy, who had encouraged me not to buy a book, he made an A on the test. I I asked, "You don't have a book and you didn't take any notes in class, how is it that you made an A on the test?" He said, "Oh, I should have told you; I have a photographic memory and the lectures and slides are really all I need because of my recall ability." Well, since I do not have a photographic memory, I bought a book and took notes. Thank You Very Much…

OK, only two more. This person I will tell you about now was one of my friends in high school. Let me tell you, he did not do anything in class, unless you count sleeping as something. Well, we all thought he was sleeping. I was definitely sure of that, since he sat by me and I would wake him up sometimes and watch the drool come out of his mouth dropping on his desk. Yuck! Our teacher was partial to multiple choice test questions and my friend, sleepyhead, would always make an A. In fact, he did well in most of his classes and all of us guys thought he was really smart.

Later, at one of my high school reunions, I asked what ever happened to our friend the sleeper? Someone said, "He went on to be a nobody, no ambition, no job, no nothing." He spent most of his time in a local bar getting drunk.

I want you to know that I saved the best for last. I became convinced that this person was a true genius. We were in the same 8th or 9th grade algebra class. (Can't remember for sure.) I think he showed up for class a day or two late carrying like four or five big books. He came down the aisle to the back of the room where I was sitting. (Alphabetical order did me no favors, it almost always put me at the back of the room.) He was wearing big, thick, reading glasses. I found out later that he had started reading books at three years old. His parents would tell him to turn out the lights and go to sleep. At which, he would grab a flashlight, go under the covers, and continue reading. This could explain why the poor eyesight and thick glasses.

Here we go again, it seemed like he never paid any attention to the teacher but would be unengaged, bored, and would start reading one of the big books he would bring to class. Talking with him was not like talking with other kids. He was always serious and straight to the point, and the things he talked about didn't interest me. It probably would today but not at 13 years old. One day, the teacher observed that he was not paying attention, and called on him to explain the algebra problem on the board. He asked her to repeat the question, as he looked up from the book he was reading. He explained how to work the problem to come up with the right answer and then he showed her a different way to work the problem to come up with the same answer. He was definitely over our heads and I believe over the teacher's head also. I do not remember her ever calling on him again that whole semester.

One day, as he sat down next to me; I noticed that he had a big thick Bible mixed in with the rest of his books. Well, OK, now I'm thinking that maybe we have something in common. As mentioned in previous letters my mom took my brother and I to church every Sunday and most Sunday nights. In fact, it wasn't an option on whether we wanted to go or not. We found out at a young age it was better to go peacefully rather than make Mom upset. So, feeling that I knew a little about the Bible, maybe we could have a friendly conversation. Thus, I began, "I see that you have a Bible with you today." To my astonishment, he responded so quickly, looked me in the face and said, "Yes, I plan to read it, to prove it's fabricated." My response was, "What does that mean?" He rolled his eyes and said, "That it's not true." WOW, this is the truth, a bad feeling came over me like something I had never felt before. I had no response to his comment. I just slumped back into my seat. We didn't talk much after that, and several weeks went by. Finally, one day I asked him if he had read from the Bible. He looked me in the eyes and said, "Yes, I've read it three times, And It's True!" It Was Like A Marvelous Sensation Came Over Me. It Was Almost Emotional, Such A Happy Feeling! When I would think about it later, I would get the same feeling all over again. I do not know what ever happened to the smart kid. As they say, maybe he went on to become a brain surgeon or a rocket scientist. After the semester was over, I do not remember ever seeing him in school again or passing him in the hall. Maybe he moved, or went straight to college from the 8th grade or something. All I know is no one has ever impressed me more than this young man…

Love,

Grandpa

Letter 15

Jude, Gabby, Fuller, Spencer, & Eve,

Hello again! I am wondering if you will ever ask yourself, "Why did Grandpa write us these letters, and what did Grandpa get out of it, by sharing his past childhood, and teenage years?" In this letter, I will try to answer this question.

Life is so short. I know at your age this probably doesn't come to mind. After all, you guys are teenagers and I'm 72 years old. As I have gotten older, I have realized that the Bible is definitely true. Pertaining to what it says in

James 4:14, you do not know what tomorrow will bring, for what is your life, but a vapor. I guess fog could be considered a vapor. How long does fog last when the sun comes up? Maybe an hour or two? James was comparing your life on earth to eternity in Heaven.

So now getting back to why I write you these letters. I wanted to help you in some of the decisions that you will face, and to avoid some of the mistakes that I made. I want you to be successful in your endeavors, whatever they may be. As I think back to when I was a teenager, my desires were to play baseball, to get a part-time job, to make money so I could buy a scooter. The plans I made as a teenager were all about now, and all about me, with little regard for the future.

About five years ago I heard a man being interviewed by a college student. His name was T. Boone Pickens, Jr., who was considered a very successful businessman worth well over a billion dollars. He had donated a lot of money to different organizations and institutions. It is said that he donated in the neighborhood of $400 million to Oklahoma State University. Also, he gave millions of dollars for medical research, building new hospitals, etc. T. Boone was born in Holdenville, Oklahoma with a population of about 5,000 people. In contrast, the population of Houston, TX and surrounding counties is about 7 million people. When the young lady asked him how he become so successful, his answer included hard work, being at the right place at the right time, and planning ahead. After high school, T. Boone Pickens, Jr. attended Oklahoma State University where he played basketball.

T. Boone gave a lot of credit to his grandmother for his success. He said that when he was twelve, and they would gather for

Thanksgiving at Grandma's house, she would ask him, "What are your plans for the spring?" His answer would be, "Grandma, I haven't even thought about it. My plans are to get ready for the basketball season and go to school." He said at Christmas his grandmother would ask him what his plans were for the summer. His response again would be, "Grandma, it's Christmas, and summer is a long time off." She would say, "Well, do you plan on having a job in the summer?" His response was, "Yes, I plan to mow lawns." She asked if he even had a lawn mower, and he said he didn't, but that he planned to buy one. She told him that he should try to find one now, rather than wait. T. Boone went on to say that his grandmother was a big part of him being successful by the advice she would give him.

I'm sure T. Boone, as president of a large corporation, asked his subordinates some of the same questions that his grandmother asked him when he was 12 years old. In summary, having a plan enhances your chances of being successful.

Love,

Grandpa

Letter 16

Jude, Gabby, Fuller, Spencer, & Eve,

"How do you mend a broken heart?" is the name of a song by The Bee Gees. In this song there is a verse, "No One Told Me About the Sorrow." This letter is about sorrow that you may experience sometime in your life. In fact, it's almost guaranteed that it will show up sooner or later.

When I was in elementary school, life for me was all about family, friends, cousins, and just hanging out and having fun. The only sorrow I experienced at that time in my life was having a stomach bug and not being able to play baseball or spend time with friends. One could say my life was just problem-free with no worries.

I remember going out for a basketball team in 5th grade. At tryouts, the coaches had us do all sorts of drills, layups, free throws, passes, etc. At the end, the head coach explained that there is a list on my door of the names of players who made the team. I must have gone over that list 3 or 4 times, but could not find my name. As a 5th grader, that indeed was a sad day for me.

I once had a dog named Rocky. Rocky was not allowed in the house and he was not on a leash, or put in a pen at night or anytime; he just ran free. One thing about Rocky: he followed me everywhere I went, especially in the summertime. When Rocky died prematurely and unexpectedly, that was definitely a sad day for me. As a kid, I really loved that dog.

When I started junior high, my Grandad died. That's what my brother and I called him, Grandad. We started spending the night with our grandparents when we were 5 or 6 years old. In the summer, we would spend a couple of weeks with them. My grandad was amazing. When spending time with him, I felt differently, and no other person could make me feel this way. He could stimulate your thinking, which is hard to explain, kind of eye opening, so to speak. He died in the basement of his church. He was working on a plumbing problem when his heart gave out, as I heard one adult explain it to another. This was so unexpected, and it affected our whole family—aunts, uncles, and all of our cousins. The notification of his death brought such grief and sadness to our home. After that, I began thinking about how death is always lurking about, with its siblings, tragedy and suffering. Many years later, my cousin was killed in a car accident. Going to the funeral of a young person is one of the most sorrowful things I've ever experienced.

To me, being engulfed with sorrow makes you feel like you're all alone. In the Bible it says if you are a child of God, He will never leave you nor forsake you. The Bible also says, "Fear Not I Will Help You." My opinion is, God's help comes when He feels you need it, not when you feel you need it. His help is always right on time. Again, I end this letter by encouraging you to read your Bible, pray and focus on others. Honor your father and your mother, and be a blessing to your siblings, teachers, coaches, and friends. Oh yeah, and your grandparents...

Grandpa

Letter 17

Jude, Gabby, Fuller, Spencer, & Eve,

Hello again. There was a time in my life when the company I worked for decided not to do business in Oklahoma anymore. In fact, this happened to me more than once. I found myself looking for a job, since mine had been terminated. While I was putting my resume together, I would sometimes take a temporary job to sustain my family needs until the job I wanted surfaced. One of my friends mentioned to me that since I had a college degree, I could substitute teach in the public school system.

I became a substitute teacher for elementary, junior high, and high school. It was actually fun and I really enjoyed it. I would say that junior high kids were the most difficult. In fact, they did the same stuff to me that my friends and I did to our sub teachers back when we were in junior high: passing notes in class, sharpening their pencil every five minutes, and asking to go to the bathroom so they could run around the halls, just to name a few.

One day a teacher approached me with the idea of driving a school bus in addition to sub teaching. This would allow me to make even more money until the right job came along. Not only was I a substitute teacher, I became a sub bus driver too. I found myself driving busloads of elementary kids, junior high kids, and high school kids. It was fun, with my biggest concern being the safety of the elementary kids. I had one junior high kid, who, as we passed his house, would toss his whole backpack out the window due to the fact that the bus stop was at the end of his block. One day as he was exiting the bus, I explained to him that when my son was in junior high, he got suspended from riding the bus for throwing a pencil out the window. I said, "Here you are, throwing your whole backpack out the window. Don't do that anymore." Some bus drivers would write kids up every week for doing something wrong while riding the bus. I was pretty lenient with my bus kids, never writing up even one kid for bad behavior, but always giving a warning. I knew that if I wrote up a kid, a copy would go to the principal, his homeroom teacher, his parents, and the bus barn. I was never in favor of zero tolerance rules or laws for that matter. The most fun I had as a bus driver was driving the girls and boys basketball teams to their games.

Kids change so much from elementary to high school. I remember in high school my brother and I sort of went in different directions. He started hanging around with the more popular kids. Even though they were a little more popular, I didn't agree with some of their behavior. I would hear about parties where some of the kids would show up with some type of alcoholic drinks and they would smoke marijuana. I told my brother that he was stupid to hang around with those guys because they would eventually end up in trouble. We were only a year apart as mentioned, and I would hear from my friends some of the stuff that my brother was involved in. I never mentioned it to my parents. If you related it to Star Wars, it was like he had defected to the dark side. My friends were some of the same friends that I had in junior high and even elementary school that I liked hanging around with and trusted. My Sunday school teacher would encourage us to ask God for help in choosing our friends. Also, he told us to continue to ask God to help choose a job, a spouse, and to always include God in decisions through prayer. Well, I must confess I didn't always do this. Why? I was afraid if God chose my girlfriend, she may be very spiritual but not very pretty or attractive. I also thought if God chose my job, it might be in the deepest part of Africa as a missionary. As an older man now, I feel that there were most likely a number of blessings that I missed out on, for not trusting God…

Well, until we meet again, please know that I think of you every day and pray that God will give you wisdom, knowledge, and understanding in life.

Grandpa

Letter 18

Jude, Gabby, Fuller, Spencer, & Eve,

Hello again! Let me start off with why I write letters to you. In these letters, I share my feelings pertaining to work, ethics, jobs I've had, sports, country, friends, family, and the most important, in my opinion, God. Why? Because I love you, and in this world we live in, it's a battle for your mind. My hope is that you will weigh the information available before making a decision. I hope that you will not be swayed by others, because you understand your job isn't to please everyone. Know both sides and the situation at hand. As a result, we are no longer to be children, tossed here and there by waves, and carried about by every wind of doctrine, by the trickery of men, by craftiness and deceitful scheming. (Ephesians 4:14) As you continue to mature and face the crossroads, or better put, critical junctures in your life, how will you know which way to turn? Who can you trust? What's best in the long run? When I was barely in my twenties, a person asked me how I felt about abortion. In the late sixties and early seventies, you were either on one side or the other. I was a freshman in college, and didn't know much about it when my parents mentioned it. A year later, it was legal in this nation.

Why would a potential mother want to kill her unborn child? For me, it's hard to comprehend. I watched the Hollywood Oscars, and I remember a young woman who had received an Oscar for her performance. As she accepted the award, she explained how it would have not been possible if she had not terminated her pregnancy. This made me very sad to think that a person would place their ambitions above the life of a helpless, unborn child. I wondered how she might feel later in life as she looks upon her trophy, knowing it represents the sacrifice of her baby.

To me, the Bible is very clear on a child in the womb. "Before I formed you in the womb I knew you, and before you were born, I consecrated you; I have appointed you a prophet to the nations." (Jeremiah 1:5)

As most of you know, I will be seventy-five years old on my next birthday. In my lifetime, there have been many changes in laws, in our values and beliefs, and in our overall culture. Let me close with this statement. Always search for the truth." I am not the only one to tell you to live a life of truth and honesty. As your grandpa, I'm ashamed of not always standing up for what I believe in. That's right, a lack of courage in the face of adversity and disputes with my friends, teachers, my supervisors, and at times even my parents. Pray for Strength, Wisdom, and Courage. A famous person one said, "Courage is rightly esteemed the first of human qualities, because it is the quality which guarantees all others." Can you show courage, humility, and love at the same time? "Take my yoke upon you and learn from me, for I am gentle, and humble in heart: and you shall find rest for your soul." (Mattew 11:29)

Yours Truly,

Grandpa

Letter 19

Jude, Gabby, Fuller, Spencer, & Eve,

Things to tell your sons when you grow up, get married, and have a family. This advice comes from your grandpa, who has 75 years of firsthand experience, who loves you, prays for you, and wants you to be successful in life.

OK here we go…"Things to tell or even teach your sons."

1. Do not enter a swimming pool by the stairs. Boys don't do that.

2. Take time to snuggle your pets, they love you so much and are always happy to see you.

3. Never be afraid to ask out the best-looking girl in the room.

4. Think twice before turning down a breath mint.

5. Eat lunch with the new kid.

6. Do not shake hands with a man or a woman while sitting down.

7. When shaking hands with someone, grip firmly and look them in the eye.

8. Thank a veteran.

9. Stand up to bullies, protect those who are being bullied.

10. After writing an angry email, read it very carefully and then delete it.

11. Give credit where credit is due. Take the blame if it is on you.

12. In a negotiation, never make the first offer.

13. Be humble and confident at the same time.

14. Return a borrowed vehicle with a full tank of gas.

15. You married the girl; you married the family.

16. Treat your wife like you want your son to treat his wife.

17. Treat your parents like you want your son to treat you.

18. Request the late checkout.

19. Do not put all your faith in mankind's prediction of the future.

20. When entrusted with a secret, keep it, or discuss with a parent or grandparent, but make sure you can trust the one you choose.

21. Hold your heroes to a higher standard no matter how talented they are.

22. Go to church. You get the world all week, you need to hear both sides.

23. Be respectful always. Acknowledge your parents and grandparents when they show up to one of your functions.

24. Never be embarrassed of one of your family members.

25. Most importantly, never be ashamed of Jesus. You would not want Jesus to be ashamed of you when show up to heaven. (Read Luke 9:26)

26. Hang with people who lead you down the right path.

27. Always search for the truth, and pray for discernment.

28. A lie can travel half way around the world, while the truth is putting on its shoes.

29. Some people will give you an ocean of truth if you will only accept a cup of lies.

30. 99% of the time the truth is very simple to understand.

31. What comes out of your mouth defines you.

32. Sincerity makes the very least person to be of more value than the most talented hypocrite.

33. No one knows who is listening; say nothing you would not want put on social media.

34. If you realize that you are of the minority, be like a duck, remain calm on the surface and paddle like crazy underneath.

35. Many men owe the grandeur of their life to the tremendous difficulties they have faced.

36. Rest assured that there is nothing new in theology, but what is false. The truth is still the truth and hasn't changed since Jesus created the Earth.

37. If you are indeed a born-again Christian and believer that the Bible is true, then you are a son of the Most High and if God is for you, who can be against you?

38. When making a decision, take it to your Heavenly Father in prayer. He may not care what color of socks you wear, but I'm sure He cares about your actions, your attitude, and the people you hang with.

39. If your sons play sports, encourage them to play with passion and dedication.

40. Tell your son not to badmouth another player on his team. As a parent you also should adhere to this advice. You run the risk of hurting the overall spirit and

success of the team. In a game, when your son hesitates to pass the ball to the bad kid that you have degraded, it's your son that looks bad. It's your son that ends up on the bench.

41. Do not share your frustrations with your kids; they just want to play and have fun.

42. Gravitate toward people who reassure you, who enlighten you, who encourage you, who comfort you, who calm you, and who convict you when you're on the wrong path.

43. Always remember that your Heavenly Father loves you. When life becomes a tough struggle, people turn their back and friends flee, what a blessed thing to see the Savior does not forsake you, but keeps you, holds you fast, clings to you, and will not let you go!!!

Remember that I try to pray for you every day…. Have a good life…

Sincerely,

Grandpa

Dear Jude, Gabby, Fuller, Spencer, & Eve,

The letter you are about to read is a summary of life from a 75-year-old grandpa's perspective. In this world, you must understand that it's a battle for your mind. Everywhere you turn it seems it's always about your needs. There are many catch phrases in the media. Some examples are, "Get what you deserve," "Pamper yourself, it's all about you." Personally, I do not believe this is a healthy way of thinking. Also, today's world is a world of isolation, with television, computers, etc. You would be right in thinking that a person does need time alone to ponder, in other words, to think about "something" before making a decision or reaching a conclusion. Time to pray that God will influence your decision, asking for His help in any situation big or small. Also, in my opinion, you should try to spend your time with things that are eternal. Most of the things we see and deal with, such as cars, houses, and computers will be obsolete in the future or will pass away completely. Now, on the other hand, people are eternal, according to the Bible. As believers, we view this as good news; to others it could be bad news. Spend time with people, be a good listener. You cannot learn if you are talking and not listening. Ask God to help you choose your companions, friends, and partners.

Because you are a citizen of the United States of America, it is most likely that you will hear a lot of talk about God. If you want to know about God, pray and read your Bible. What can I tell you? Well, God is God, who can say to Him, "What are you doing?" You may say, "If I were a believer in Christ Jesus, how should I live my life in this present world?" I would encourage you to read Romans Chapter 12:9-21. After you read this, know that the Bible contains other verses that may help you succeed in life. An example would be, if you are going out of town to play a basketball game, football, soccer, tennis match, or a pickleball tournament, you might want to pray as Jabez did. Read 1 Chronicles 4:9. You may ask, why do people praise and give thanks to God? Throughout the Bible, we find many reasons to worship, praise, and thank God. Believers thank God for all that He has done, for all the He is doing, and for all that He will do in the future. We praise God for His Holiness, Psalms 30:4. We praise God for His Mercy, Psalms 136:26. We praise God for His mighty works, Isaiah 25:1. We worship God because He is the Great Creator, Revelation 4:11. We worship God and give praise to God because He has given us Salvation, 2 Thessalonians 2:13. We praise God for the Grace that He has given us through Jesus Christ, 1st Corinthians 1:4. We give thanks to God always for everything, Ephesians 5:20.

You know I have three citizenships. I am a citizen of the Cherokee Nation. I am a citizen of the United States of America. I have a citizenship in Heaven, Philippians 3:20. My citizenship in heaven is not because of what I have done, BUT because of what my Lord did on The Cross, 1 Corinthians 15:1-4. For God so loved the world, that he gave his only begotten son that whosoever believeth in him should not perish but have everlasting life,

John 3:16. For God the Father did not send his only begotten son into the world to condemn the world, but that the world through Him might be saved, John 3:17.

In closing, remember your Creator in the days of your youth. The Wisest man who ever lived on the earth sums it up in two verses. Please read Ecclesiastes 12:13-14. In the Bible, Samson poses a riddle to his groomsmen. See Judges 14:12-19. Let me present a conundrum to you: "What Can Be Swallowed or Can Swallow a Person?"

If you wake up one day in the future and a lot of people are missing, just remember that you still have a chance.

Yours truly,

Grandpa

Answer: to Grandpa's Conundrum…(P R I D E)

Family Photos

Grandad Andy Reece (far right) and his brothers.

Grandad Andy Reece in his later years, at church.

Grandpa Tim Weaver and Nana
Barbara Weaver and family